The Politician's Essential
EXCUSE BOOK

The Politician's Essential

EXCUSE BOOK

Andrew Murray Howe V

This book is dedicated to my great-grandfather, Andrew "Murray" Howe II, my cousin, Bryn Lewis, and the detention room chalkboard at the beginning of *The Simpsons*, which contains some of the most eloquent political punditry ever scrawled by Bart Simpson: fifty times each.

DISCLAIMER: While these excuses are both humorous and accurate, they do NOT usually form the basis for legal defense when a candidate is arrested, indicted, prosecuted, and otherwise accused – although they certainly bear an uncanny resemblance to the pleas many politicians have employed in court: you have been warned.

About

A compendium of sure-fire excuses for any candidate who is down in the polls, makes that unfortunate gaffe, needs to energize a lagging campaign, or has the temerity to actually lose an election. A must-have for politicians, pundits, campaign staffers, volunteers, and voters of every party. It is recommended to be applied anytime the press will be within two miles of your candidate.

Excuses are numbered for easy reference, and ample space has been provided to modify each excuse to fit your candidate's actual current crisis.

Foreword

In 1904, my great-grandfather, a horse racing Hall of Fame photojournalist, wrote *The Trottin Hoss EXCUSE BOOK*, a pocket guide of humorous explanations for the loss of a horse race. His book remains a classic in racing circles to this day, as the excuses have proved timeless. It is still available in the Harness Racing Museum and Hall of Fame in Goshen, New York, both online and as a premium for membership in the museum.

The similarities of politics to horse racing are uncanny, the venerable horse race bearing a remarkable resemblance to political races large and small, without regard to party affiliation or after-party parties. Thus, several of his racing excuses are readily adapted herein, and the final excuse is virtually verbatim.

Scrawl your own spin here:

No. 1
The candidate was not properly prepared by staff
Aka
[Who let him/her near a microphone untended?]

This phrase is a good catch-all but best pulled out during
debate season when your candidate refers to Pakistan as a
suburb of East LA, or the "*Feral* Trade Commission" as a
tax on Chinese gym shoes.

No. 2
Our supporters were barred from the polls
Aka
[We didn't know where to vote]

Use this gem when someone driving a car with your
candidate's bumper sticker is arrested after crashing
through a fast food restaurant lobby while smoking crack
as the polls open on Election Day.

Scrawl your own spin here:

No. 3
We don't pay attention to polls
Aka
[When those polls are killing us]

*Use this phrase in many circumstances including when
your candidate drops twenty-six points in all polls after it
is discovered he paid the woman next door to take a urine
drug test for him – and the lab results came back that he
is pregnant.*

No. 4
A week is a lifetime in politics
Aka
[Don't use at the Senior Citizen rally]

*This is a quick aphorism to apply when a week before the
election, your candidate's campaign headquarters phones
have been shut off due to non-payment and the papers
stop mentioning your candidate in the tracking polls
because they can't find him/her in any of them.*

Scrawl your own spin here:

No. 5
Venue did not favor our candidate
Aka
[The audience were jerks]

Invented by Noah when his pet camel lost a race to Ham's
dromedary on the swampy side of Mount Ararat just after
the ark landed. Use it whenever you can't think of a better
excuse for the blogs claiming your candidate lost a debate,
even when that candidate was running unopposed.

No. 6
The press is biased against us
Aka
[They keep printing my record]

Dig up this gem when a debate transcript is published in
every major newspaper, and negative comments about
your candidate outweigh the positive comments by a
margin of Washington to Nixon.

Scrawl your own spin here:

No. 7
The candidate had food poisoning
Aka
[Did the candidate just mix Ambien with Jagermeister?]

Use when your candidate is found passed out in the unisex bathroom of a French restaurant and swears that "Marilyn Monroe bought me the drinks."

No. 8
Opponent is taking political advantage of a crisis
Aka
[My husband/wife/other is releasing our divorce/paternity/IRS/sex tape]

Use this essential screen when your candidate is down in the polls but your opponent's house catches fire, and the six o'clock news shows your opponent's family dousing the flames with fire extinguishers in their pajamas.

Scrawl your own spin here:

No. 9
Opponent abused elected office for campaign purposes
Aka
[Just wait till I'M elected...]

Fire this one when your incumbent opponent shows up at any function, political or otherwise, and is introduced with his/her/other's title of office in front of their name.

No. 10
Opponent is pandering
Aka
[No fair to pander when I'm doing it too]

Use when your candidate's opponent shows up at a Town Hall Meeting and thanks the audience for attending.

Scrawl your own spin here:

No. 11
Opponent is pandering to the right

Use when your candidate's opponent ends a speech with
"God Bless America."

No. 12
Opponent is pandering to the left

Use when your candidate's opponent starts a speech with
"My Fellow Americans."

Scrawl your own spin here:

No. 13
Opponent is using attack ads, slinging mud
Aka
[How did they find out all that true stuff?]

A limited but effective excuse – only use on a day when
your candidate's attack ads don't run as often as your
opponent's attack ads due to a change in daylight savings
time in your candidate's time zone, which is different from
your opponent's time zone.

No. 14
We support all hard-working constituents

Use when your candidate is shown on the news exiting a
"Gentlemen's Club" with two "Pole Workers."

Scrawl your own spin here:

No. 15
Opponent supports out of control spending

Use when your opponent's unbalanced budget includes
expenditures that don't benefit your candidate's base vs.
your candidate's unbalanced budget, which does.

No. 16
Opponent does not have foreign policy experience
Aka
[Unlike me, who has hired many
undocumented aliens]

Use when your opponent's family vacations in Florida,
while your candidate's family vacations in the Bahamas.

Scrawl your own spin here:

No. 17
Candidate was misquoted
Aka
[By himself]

Use when your candidate is quoted in every major paper as
saying "American cars are inferior," rather than,
"American cars are inferior to foreign cars."

No. 18
Candidate's comments taken out of context
Aka
[By himself]

Great when your candidate says on an accidental open
microphone: "My opponent is a lying, cheating, draft
dodging, tax evading SOB," but misses the off-microphone
portion: "and is a raging alcoholic."

Scrawl your own spin here:

No. 19
We were snake-bit
Aka
[By a real snake]

Use when your incumbent candidate loses a fixed race in their home district. To a family member.

No. 20
We were unlucky
Aka
[To have such an idiot for a candidate]

Use when your candidate finishes second in a two-candidate field four times running.

Scrawl your own spin here:

No. 21
Expectations were too high
Aka
[After all, who doesn't occasionally drool in public?]

Use when your candidate loses a national election so badly that the next year he/she is not a viable candidate for town council. In Brazil.

No. 22
The candidate was caught off guard

Use when your candidate is asked for their position on Medicare and responds with an explanation of global warming.

Scrawl your own spin here:

No. 23
Opponent is a liar
Aka
[It takes one to know one]

This classic dates back to ancient Mesopotamia, and is suitable for all occasions where your opponent's opinion differs from your candidate's, but has proven more popular in the blogs.

No. 24
Opponent won on name recognition
Aka
[Even when that name is unpronounceable]

Use when your candidate Luciana Pinkelworth loses by twenty-six points to John Smith.

Scrawl your own spin here:

No. 25
Political climate was not right
Aka
[Candidate was overly-global-warmed]

Use after a loss when your candidate's central campaign platform to "ban all pets and foreigners – and foreigner's pets" fails to garner any voter support whatsoever.

No. 26
Opponent is soft on immigration
Aka
[Charmin cuddly soft on immigration]

Essential for use when your candidate's operatives discover your opponent has an illegal alien nanny, but only after your candidate's illegal alien gardener formally accepts a position with the next-door neighbor at minimum wage for the higher pay.

Scrawl your own spin here:

No. 27
Opponent is in the pocket of big industry
Aka
[And it's a pocket full of cash]

Use when [insert Fortune 500 name here] fails to pay up to
your own candidate's Super PAC as promised.

No. 28
Hit below the belt
Aka
[No fair taking my words in context]

Use when in the second debate your opponent quotes
verbatim your candidate's position from the first debate.

Scrawl your own spin here:

No. 29
Our base is grassroots
Aka
[Our supporters are raised free range]

Apply when your candidate's immediate family is the sole
group that allows your candidate's yard signs in front of
their houses.

No. 30
Weather negatively influenced voter turnout for
our candidate
Aka
[Our voters are afraid of light]

Use after a close loss on a day when the blue sky is so
blinding that no one will venture out without sunglasses.

Scrawl your own spin here:

No. 31
Opponent played dirty politics
Aka
[Why didn't we think up all that great stuff?]

Use with care as this rarely happens.

No. 32
Candidate was tired
Aka
[When the candidate keeps referring/slurring to his "real" running mate: the Honorable Jack Daniels]

Use when your candidate staggers and falls on the way to the podium, knocking over twelve American flags into six orphans in the front row who have to be removed on stretchers with minor injuries, and declines a sobriety test because it's "Under-American."

Scrawl your own spin here:

No. 33
Voter fraud cost us the election
Aka
[We need to learn to cheat better]

Use when one of your poll watchers follows a voter home, and finds your opponent's yard sign in front of the voter's house and your candidate's bumper sticker on the car the voter is driving.

No. 34
Opponent out of touch with ordinary Americans
Aka
[Our guy sees MANY, MANY ordinary Americans from his limo]

Use when one of your candidate's political operatives secretly films your opponent buying mouthwash at one store, when it is advertised on sale across town.

Scrawl your own spin here:

No. 35
Opponent does not support American made products
Aka
[ARE there any more American made products?]

Employ when your candidate's foreign luxury car is in the shop and your candidate is filmed in an American luxury car loaner, while your opponent is filmed by an operative driving their own foreign luxury car.

No. 36
They outspent us
Aka
[His parents' trust fund is bigger than our guy's parents' trust fund]

Use when a seven-figure check from your candidate's Super PAC bounces to Steubenville and back and your candidate is forced to fly coach for three weeks.

Scrawl your own spin here:

No. 37
We are surging in the polls
Aka
[Somebody actually recognized our guy]

Use when your candidate is double-digit-down in the polls
with a three-point margin of error, and your candidate's
staff adds the three points to your side of the ledger just to
improve staff morale.

No. 38
Opponent is an elitist
Aka
[He finished college and everything]

Use when your opponent's Ivy League school costs more
than your candidate's Ivy League school and your
opponent's hyper-exclusive country club has a higher
admission fee than your candidate's uber-exclusive
country club.

Scrawl your own spin here:

No. 39
Opponent played the race card
Aka
[His shade of white is whiter than our shade of white]

Use when your candidate is down in the polls and your opponent is a different race, is photographed with someone of a different race, or attends a major league sporting event where someone of a different race is also in the sports arena.

No. 40
We have a major announcement next week
Aka
[Even our minor announcements are major]

Apply when down in the polls and your candidate's spouse decides to go holiday shopping early to "stimulate somebody's damn economy."

Scrawl your own spin here:

No. 41
Opponent is a flip flopper
Aka
[We tried to take both sides of every issue first]

Use between debates when your opponent changes
positions on six major issues and your candidate only
changes five.

No. 42
Opponent hid their records
Aka
[Behind our records]

Use when your candidate is down in the polls and a
Freedom of Information Act request fails to yield your
opponent's kindergarten tardy record, or intramural
volleyball team record.

Scrawl your own spin here:

No. 43
Campaign was mismanaged
Aka
[We picked the wrong candidate...again]

Open up when your candidate cannot raise enough funds
to buy bumper stickers, or enough signatures to be
included on the ballot, and their family is quoted in the
paper as voting for your opponent.

No. 44
Opponent lied about their record
Aka
[The real record is even better than they say]

Use when your opponent claims a 3.8 GPA in college, but
you discover that your opponent's GPA was actually 3.9.

Scrawl your own spin here:

No. 45
We are about to announce a major endorsement
Aka
[We're really tired of announcing minor endorsements]

Use when your candidate's local animal shelter allows your candidate's yard sign to be placed in their parking lot after adopting a puppy.

No. 46
Opponent forcing a radical agenda
Aka
[It's REALLY radical because we didn't think of it first]

Apply when down in the polls and your opponent vows to protect seniors' rights and enforce child labor laws.

Scrawl your own spin here:

No. 47
Opponent consistently proven wrong on the facts
Aka
[We only use "faith-based" facts]

Appropriate when PolitiFact gives your opponent
twenty-six "Pants on Fire" ratings and your candidate only
has twenty-five "Pants on Fire" ratings.

No. 48
Opponent cost us jobs
Aka
[His/her illegal workers are taking jobs from our illegal workers]

Use when your opponent's general contractor completes
construction of their family home and the general
contractor lays off the laborer who swept the floors on
weekends after completion.

Scrawl your own spin here:

No. 49
We are the job creators
Aka
[We hired a lot of campaign workers, didn't we?]

Use when stagnant in polls and your incumbent
candidate's office replaces a retired administrative
assistant after beginning to advertise for the position two
months before the campaign started.

No. 50
Opponent does not support the military
Aka
[Until we finally get tough on Canada]

Use when down in the polls and your opponent's flag at
home on Memorial Day is smaller than your candidate's
flag at home on Memorial Day (size matters).

Scrawl your own spin here:

No. 51
Opponent is soft on crime
Aka
[Otherwise, she/he would have already had me arrested]

Use when one of your operatives discovers that your opponent was issued a parking ticket while double parked rushing daughter to the emergency room with contractions three seconds apart.

No. 52
Opponent did not lower the price of gasoline
Aka
[Guess what it costs to fill my Bentley]

Use when down in the polls against any national incumbent at any time. Note: "lower the price of gasoline" can be replaced with "change the weather" if it was a heavy hurricane season.

Scrawl your own spin here:

No. 53
This is a Game Changer
Aka
[Not a Diaper Changer]

Employ when your candidate is down twelve points in the polls a month before the election and decides to change party affiliation.

No. 54
Ballot was confusing
Aka
[Sooo many Irish names]

Use this when your candidate named Zumstein loses the election by eighteen points and the candidates are listed in alphabetical order on the ballot.

Scrawl your own spin here:

No. 55
Opponent is soft on drugs
Aka
[I should know]

Use to attack your opponent when your opponent admits
to smoking pot in high school and didn't give you a hit.

No. 56
Opponent would use drug laws to profile
minorities and students
Aka
[He/she is trying to get their kids out of the
house]

Use to defend your candidate when your candidate admits
to smoking pot in high school.

Scrawl your own spin here:

No. 57
Opponent attacked us rather than discussing issues
Aka
[And those answers are MUCH harder to memorize]

All-purpose excuse during debate season.
Use any time your candidate was asked a question during a debate by your opponent.

No. 58
Candidate not acclimated
Aka
[Can I hide behind this podium?]

Apply when your candidate is trounced in a debate held in your candidate's home town, hosted by your own party, with an audience hand-picked by your staff.

Scrawl your own spin here:

No. 59
Our position on abortion is [insert wrong
answer here]
Aka
[Let the screaming begin...]

Use when it has been a slow week in the polls and your
candidate is just in a plain ole fightin' mood – with half of
your candidate's electorate.

No. 60
Opponent slandered military record
Aka
[I kept Cleveland safe from communism]

Use when your candidate's quasi-military service has been
observed for precisely what it was.

Scrawl your own spin here:

No. 61
Nooooo commmmennnnnnnnnnnttttt
Aka
[Nooooo commmmmennntt]

Employed when your candidate causes a multi-car pileup
after a boozy fundraiser, refuses a sobriety test, tries to kiss
the female cop, and is interviewed at the scene by a
television news team.

No. 62
No comment
Aka
[See Excuse 61]

Used by your candidate the day after causing multi-car
pileup after boozy fundraiser, re-refuses a sobriety test, is
being interviewed at campaign headquarters by a televised
news team, and tries to kiss the reporter.

Scrawl your own spin here:

No. 63
We surround ourselves with a team of qualified people
Aka
[It's all relative]

Use when one of your opponent's political operatives exposes that sixteen of your incumbent candidate's relatives, donors, business associates, and friends have been given appointed positions in your candidate's administration.

No. 64
They played cronyism
Aka
[They hired my grandmother]

Use when one of your candidate's political operatives discovers that an unpaid intern position on your incumbent opponent's staff is held by a sixth cousin twice removed.

Scrawl your own spin here:

No. 65
We make the tough decisions
Aka
[With our collective IQ, EVERY decision is a tough one]

Use to shake up the polls when your incumbent candidate approves a budget measure to repair potholes.

No. 66
Opponent playing politics with the electorate
Aka
[No fair talking to people]

Use when your candidate sinks in the polls and your opponent makes a statement to the press, debates your candidate, gives an interview, or is written about.

Scrawl your own spin here:

No. 67
Opponent is promising the sky
Aka
[He/she/it is literally promising the real sky]

Use when your opponent's campaign promises to balance the budget, end poverty, lower unemployment to zero, and achieve world peace proves more popular in the polls than your candidate's campaign promises to balance the budget, end poverty, lower unemployment to zero, and achieve world peace – their first day in office.

Scrawl your own spin here:

No. 68
My investments are in a blind trust
Aka
[The trust fund mom wouldn't let me touch]

Use when the press discovers that your candidate's
offshore accounts have been involved in a money
laundering scandal by your candidate's brother-in-law,
who has cataracts.

No. 69
Candidate was understaffed
Aka
[Where's the sock?]

Use when your staff is too small to have someone ready to
shut up the candidate at all times.

Scrawl your own spin here:

No. 70
We support gay rights
Aka
[Except for THOSE people]

Quickly distribute when your candidate is taped agreeing
with a top donor that "separate public restrooms for
homosexuals is a great idea" and it gets a lot of
play in the press.

No. 71
This is the candidate of inclusion
Aka
*[I wouldn't belong to any club that would have
me as a member]*

Use when the press reveals that your candidate's largest
donor has broken thirty-six federal election laws by
providing the funds for each of his underage factory
workers in China to give your candidate $5,000 campaign
contribution checks.

Scrawl your own spin here:

No. 72
Candidate's family should not be an issue in this campaign
Aka
[Take my wife/husband/other, please]

Use when during a high-profile fundraiser your candidate's spouse is secretly filmed by your opponent's operative punching a waiter, puking on a donor's shoes, kicking a puppy, and afterwards rear-ending a police cruiser while traveling the wrong direction on the expressway in the family station wagon at three a.m.

Scrawl your own spin here:

No. 73
We did not get our progressive message across
Aka
[Just make sure they spell my name right]

Use when Matt Drudge does not report anything with a
snarky negative headline about your candidate on
The Drudge Report during the entire campaign.

No. 74
We did not get our conservative message across
Aka
[See Excuse 73]

Use when Bill Maher does not report anything with a
snarky negative headline about your candidate on
Real Time with Bill Maher during the entire campaign.

Scrawl your own spin here:

No. 75
There is ZERO evidence that it is NOT true
Aka
[Where's The Beef?]

Use when criticized in the press for publishing a YouTube video that accuses your incumbent opponent of being responsible for the entire national debt, stock market valuations in Uzbekistan, faking the Apollo Moon Landings and Solar Flares.

No. 76
Our opponent's policies have caused a loss of public trust in the banking system
Aka
[No, those aren't Playboy Magazines under my mattress]

Use when your candidate is secretly taped by the FBI accepting $2,000,000 in unmarked bills prior to a crucial legislative vote.

Scrawl your own spin here:

No. 77
The better candidate won
Aka
[Only if we won. If not, screw them]

The absolute worst excuse ever. Although it is rumored to have been around since the early days of political races in Athens, I cannot find an example of it actually having been used. Don't even think about using it until your candidate loses seven straight races to the same opponent.

No. 78
Ain't got no excuse
Aka
[Except all the ones prior to this one]

Use at your own peril. It might pre-judge your interest in a career or civic duty that is taking your mind off your troubles and bringing you good health, happiness, and a long list of congenial friends.

POLLS CLOSED
Aka
[You don't have to go home but
you can't stay here]

Coming Soon

If you think you've seen the last of The Essential EXCUSE BOOKS, we blurt out loudly Not So! In the nearby and humorous future, stay tuned for *The Physician's Essential EXCUSE BOOK, The Attorney's Essential EXCUSE BOOK, The Parent's Essential EXCUSE BOOK* and more titles devoted to sports, dating, food, travel, hobbies, sex (almost kidding), life, death, photosynthesis (just kidding), and the Cheeses of Nazareth (Really kidding about that last one). Check in for the latest developments on our new website: *www.ExcuseBooks.com*. Sign up for our newsletter and participate in our state-of-the-art interactive Excuse Generators and Contests. *www.ExcuseBooks.com* is your best excuse, now and forever. Excuse us.

About the Author

Andrew Howe grew up one small excuse north of Cincinnati in the small town of Wyoming, Ohio. He now resides in Florida, where he is a thriving real estate developer (cranewoods.com), project consultant and "distressed project fixer." Andy is cursed with a smart#ss sense of humor (which comes in handy when discussing politics). His daughter's dog, Bambi, approved this message, but just barely.